Wildschooling:
Guide for Radical Unschooling and Conscious Parenting

By: Brittany Horton

"Most people don't get out of bed in the morning in the mood for a "learning experience", I try to wake up every day in the mood for life. Children also do this - unless they are sick or life has been made overly stressful or confusing for them. Unschooling is a unique opportunity for our family to do whatever makes sense for our personal growth and development. It's like watching a little garden grow. No matter how closely you watch your garden, it is difficult to verify that anything is happening at that very moment. But with the changing of the seasons we can see that much has happened, quietly and naturally. All we have to do is trust in the inevitability of this very organic process, and to facilitate that growth."

-Brittany Horton

TABLE OF CONTENTS

WHAT WILDSCHOOLING MEANS TO ME

Essentially we are nature based unschoolers with a profound love for art and nature. I'm going to talk a lot about unschooling in this book and what that is. Wildschooling, Unschooling, Worldschooling, Life Learning has become not just a method of homeschooling but a way of life for us. Wildschooling to me is unschooling meets shamanism, dance meets art, adventure meets the four elements. Wildschooling promotes the wild spirit, and encourages the rousing of the inner fires and creative expression beyond crayons and watercolor.

Wildschooling not only encourages an awakening of the unchained inner self, but also nurtures it and enlightens it to be bold and brave when facing both the terrestrial and mystical worlds. Is what we are doing any different than any other homeschooling family?

We do linear work, we do creative work, we seek out nature. Just like any other homeschooling or unschooling family. So, what makes us Wildschoolers? Maybe we're not too entirely different. In the same way that stretching extends the muscles and yoga extends and awakens the muscles and the soul, our intention is what is important. I want to give my girls something full bodied and all encompassing. I want to give them something beyond school, beyond learning. I want to make nature, their spirit, their inherent wildness, just as much a part of their curriculum and their lives as reading, writing, and math. If you are looking for resources, information, and inspiration for your earth-based unschooling and conscious parenting, I'm hoping this book will help.

WHY UNSCHOOLING?

"By nature people are learning animals. Birds fly; fish swim; humans think and learn. Therefore, we do not need to motivate children into leaning by wheeling, bribing, or bullying. We do not need to keep picking away at their minds to make sure they are learning. What we need to do – and all we need to do – is to give children as much help and guidance as they need and ask for, listen respectfully when they feel like talking, and then get out of the way. We can trust them to do the rest."

-John Holt, *How Children Learn*

As a parent there is nothing I get asked about more than unschooling. My husband and I have been unschooling our two wildflowers for two years now. Many of us who are considering, beginning, or transitioning to unschooling are learning as we go/grow. We definitely don't have it all figured out, but acknowledging that we're somewhere in between knowing what we're doing and knowing absolutely nothing can make a difference in feeling confident about moving forward with our vision.

Asking questions and hearing other people's journeys can be really helpful. I realize in my own process that being able to answer WHY I want to explore unschooling strongly informs HOW I want to go about it with Wildschooling. Seems simple enough, but it was only after many conversations with both supporters and skeptics that I began to see the correlation. One mom, after listening to my ideas, asked me why would I want to "radically unschool" because we live in an area that already has some well-established homeschool communities. At the time I didn't have the words to respond because I hadn't yet identified my why.

Now I know that for me, this Wildschooling journey entails more than I ever imagined and absolutely brings me joy! Building systems, discovering methodologies, and innovating practices alongside my children is a passion for me and it will always feel valuable to me when it comes to learning how my children learn. Also, I think it's healthy and natural to keep evolving. I'm a new mom, my children are young. The mom's who are connecting with me in these talks have little ones too. As families raising our children together, it's our time to start a new learning process that reflects our children's needs.

But I'm getting ahead of myself: what is unschooling? First, it's a form of homeschooling. In unschooling life itself is learning. There is no "doing school". Learning happens naturally all of the time. This is what unschooling means to me in contrast to school. Schools have goals set by teachers and the school system, the unschooler has set his or her own goals. The Wildschooler thrives through nature and creativity.

While school has specific textbooks, worksheets, or learning materials, unschoolers learn from anything – books they find, things on the Internet, siblings or parents, people working in interesting fields, traveling, museums, anything. As Wildschoolers we do a lot of our learning outdoors. School is structured and unschooling changes with your child. Children in school learn how to follow instructions, unschoolers learn to think for themselves and make their own decisions.

Schooled children are expected to learn at a pace arbitrarily set by administrators and unschoolers learn at their own pace. In school learning happens at certain times in the classroom and in unschooling learning happens all of the time and there is no separation between learning and life. Unschoolers learn just like you or I learn as adults: based on what interests them and figuring out how to learn it on their own and driven by curiosity and practical application rather than because someone says it's important. This is how I learn as a self taught artist and a self employed writer, as an entrepreneur, and as a parent.

Sometimes the word "unschool" isn't completely accurate in my opinion, which is why we like the term Wildschooling so much. What I am dreaming up is a family-centered, individualized, series of adventures that engages the whole family, creatively and spiritually. I'm still mapping this out and finding the words! It's hard to explain why we unschool without generalizing. Ultimately, it's the little things, the big ah-ha moments like the first words your child will read. It's the things we take for granted, the morning snuggles, the days unfolding naturally and slowly. It's freedom. Freedom to play, explore, take risks, make mistakes, learn, and grow.

Personalized and consensual learning is true happiness when children have the freedom to learn what they want and explore their interests and talents. Unschooling gives children the freedom that allows them to master things, and to fail and try again without pressure. Unschooling embraces and celebrates family and relationships are nourished and developed all of the time. Unschooled life is a deliberate life filled with authentic friendships and socialization with people of all ages. Unschooling is time. It's time to be bored, to tinker, to daydream. Unschooling is time to play, and play, and play! Unschooled children are free! They are free from pressure and free from conformity.

Our Wildschoolers say that life for them is like best Saturday ever for their schooled friends... the day that kids dream about when they are stuck in school.

HOW TO UNSCHOOL

There is no right or wrong way to do it, no single way. Parents who are new to this always want to know how to do it. We did and we're still figuring it out. Why is there no answer? Because every kid is different. Everyone has different needs, interests, abilities, goals, and environments. What would you say if people told you there was only one way to live your life, one way to do your job? You'd hate it, because it would take away your freedom, and also all the fun. Telling you how to unschool is like taking away your freedom and all the fun out of it. The questions are everything, and the finding out is the fun part. With that said, I will offer some ideas of how we unschool, and some ideas of how you might approach things, but these are just ideas to start you out!

Fairies, mermaids, dragons, and all things fantasy. Our 8-year-old loves to play fantasy games and read about mermaids. Often she will pretend she is one. Also a fairy or a super hero. She likes to draw pictures and read with us and make up stories. She's pretty good at math on her own, though we don't really study that with her much. Aside from the fantasy world she is also really interested in science. Our house stays covered in paint, glue, slime, and glitter.

Our 3-year-old likes to be read to and even loves to try and read on her own. She's been learning to read through games and reading with us. She likes colors and tries to write her name. She makes forts and art and likes to play outside and pretend play as everything from a mermaid to a doctor.

The power of questions. When the kids ask a question, that's an opportunity to find out something. We'll look it up together, or look for books on it in the library, at the used book store, or on Amazon. People you know are incredible resources. If your kid wants to be a chef, you might know someone who is a chef or owns a restaurant. If your kid wants to create games, you might know a programmer. If your kid is interested in science, you might know a marine biologist. And so on. Connect them with these people.

Games are your best friend. Play all kinds of games. Don't be concerned with what they're learning. They'll have fun, and learn that life can be play, and so can learning.

Our children are immersed in the arts at the moment so I've been taking them to every art show in town and they are involved in dance and our local community theater. They've been meeting people, gaining inspiration, and have opportunities now for voice and piano lessons. Networking with your community is key.

If you're new to unschooling, it's a good idea to deschool. This can take a couple weeks, a couple months. The idea is to get them (and you) out of the mindset of schooling, which can be very difficult, because we've been trained to think in terms of school. We think we need to be productive teachers and students, and that school has to be done a certain way, and that if the kids aren't learning something from an activity, it has no value. Expose them.

Have books and magazines lying around the house, watch shows about interesting things, get out and explore your town, meet different people, find stuff together on the Internet. This exposure will help them to explore new interests. Even if they don't seem interested at first, the exposure will allow them to find new things on their own. Play. Make things. Learn as you go. Try different things. Go out and do things, meet people, have fun learning about new things. Have fun, always have fun. Never force, always get pulled. Be patient. As your child learns that learning is fun and can be done all the time in lots of ways the learning will happen. When you get frustrated that your child doesn't want to read or write, instead let them play music, read comic books, or play outside.

WHY CHILDREN NEED NATURE

"Now I see the secret of the making of the best persons, It is to grow in the open air and to eat and sleep with the earth." -Walt Whitman

Whitman wrote these words almost two-hundred years ago, though their importance is more relevant than ever. The call of technology attracts children to come inside, to stare at glowing screens, to spend precious time playing video games. It is a telling example that my 8-year-old daughter knows more about computers than I do. I think technology is great and we actually do not have a limit for screen time. With that being said I see first hand the way my children respond when they experience nature. It is as if the entrapment of their sophisticated lives fall away, and even to them, the conversation of video games seems out of place. Every time I bring my kids into the woods I am reminded that nature, the cool breeze, the feel of crisp Autumn leaves under our feet, the smell of pine, the sound of water flowing peacefully has not lost its power.

To me, nature is our classroom full of endless possibilities, with lessons ready to be learned, and answers to all of our deepest questions. I grew up out in nature. It has always felt like my REAL home and is the one place where I am able to let go and forget all of my outside worries. Some of my fondest memories are set in the woods behind my childhood home, where I climbed trees, built dams and forts, and chased fireflies until the night darkened. Unfortunately, many young children today do not have as many direct experiences with nature. This disconnect from the natural world is producing ill effects in both the minds and bodies of young people, but I'm optimistic that well-intentioned, forward-thinking parents and facilitators can close the kid-nature gap.

As humans, we have an affinity for the natural world. Therefore, a connection to nature is biologically innate. Children miss out when they spend most of their time indoors. Problems associated with alienation from nature include depression, obesity, and attention deficit disorder. Kids who have direct access to nature are better learners. Exposure to nature has been shown to reduce stress and increase attention spans. When a child is experiencing nature, all the senses are activated. Immersion in something bigger than themselves, rather than focusing narrowly on one thing, such as a computer screen. They're seeing, hearing, touching, tasting. Out in nature, a child's brain has the chance to rejuvenate, so the next time they need to focus and pay attention, they will be more aware. Even if kids don't have any of the specific problems mentioned above, kids who don't get out much lack the sense of wonder that only nature can provide.

NURTURING YOUR CHILD'S INTUITION

All children are naturally intuitive. From the moment they first enter the physical world, they rely on their sixth sense for communication and protection. It is what they innately know. They rely on these primary unsaid feelings for day-to-day survival before speech, mental, and social skills have developed. Our sixth sense is natural and part of who we are. Maybe we think about somebody and they call us? Maybe we meet somebody and we can't quite put our finger on it, but they feel a bit familiar. We all start out as babies with an intuitive sense. What we do with it – and how we choose to use it or not use it – is where we differ. As we grow older, we develop confining beliefs based on our experiences or the response we get from the world around us. Trusting yourself, being self-aware, and leading by example is the best thing you can do to help your child. If you can trust yourself and know your own worth, then listening to what you want becomes very natural. Here are some practical tips that you might like to to try.

Stay in touch with your inner voice. This is the one that talks to you, not to be confused with your inner critic. Learn to distinguish between your inner critic and your own loving gentle voice. Ensure your child's inner voice is full of positivity too. Watch the way you reflect back to them how they are. It's true that if you are harsh on yourself, you will be harsh on others too. Tell them what you love about them on a daily basis and acknowledge positive behaviors.

Connect with your heart. We often make decisions with our logic so they are based on our limited experience of the world. Next time you need to make a decision, put your hand over your heart and take a deep breath. Listening to your head and your heart is crucial to good decision-making about your life. You can do this out loud so your children are witnesses to some of the decisions you make and you can use this when they are making decisions. Ask them, 'What would your heart say?' Take a deep breath in, close your eyes and see what the answer is.

Connect with your body. The mind and body connection is so strong. You can even create illnesses in our body by the thoughts we think. An example is that when my depression reemerges I feel sick to my stomach. Believe it or not, the stomach problems are because something is literally 'eating me' and I was holding onto something in the past or not letting go of something. Your gut health and your emotions are so closely linked, it is fair to say that the gut acts as a sort of primitive brain. Butterflies or nausea are often your inner truth speaking to you. You may want to consider keeping a journal of your symptoms to help you clarify factors associated with your symptoms. I also have used meditation in the past and I make more sensible food choices. Mindfulness breathing and relaxation is something I do with my daughters. It releases the same chemicals into your brain that a big hug would. It's just as soothing as a hug to sit there quietly and breathe deeply from your stomach for 10 minutes a day.

Encourage creativity. Allow your children to just be. Let them play, make things, discover and grow. Nourish their souls with creativity. Creativity does actually belong to children. Creativity allows children to be playful, authentic and come from a place that is not limited or conditioned. Make time to be creative for yourself and with your children. It doesn't have to be loads of crafts and messiness if you don't have time. It can simply be a game or making tea together. Great things happen when you get creative. Your subconscious takes over and shows you exactly what you are made of.

Take care of yourself. I cannot stress how important it is to learn to love yourself. Understand that self-love is not selfish and that if you are not taken care of, you will be no good to anybody else.

Teaching our children to be kind and put others first is something most parents teach their children growing up. However, it's also important to teach your child that they are not responsible for other people's happiness. Phrases such as 'That makes me happy' or 'If you don't that so and so will be sad' sends out a message that it is their job to make other people happy. Teach them that it's OK to say 'no' to anybody including adults if you don't want to do something. They need to honor and respect no from other people as well being able to say it!

Validate. Encourage your child to trust their own judgment. When they come to you and tell you about something that makes them feel bad, no matter how trivial or how much you disagree, validate it for them. They cannot do this for themselves and they rely heavily on you to reflect back to them what the world looks like.

CREATIVITY BELONGS TO CHILDREN

Teach your children about art and on their intuition and creativity, and less on technique. When very young children start playing with toys and crayons they listen to and trust themselves. They follow their instincts and their urge to explore the vast world in which they have just arrived. They seem to flow with the inner current of their creativity, and with amazing freedom. When coming from a pure place, children create only for the sake of play and for the thrill of inventing, never for a proposed result. They create from the center of their being, an authentic place, unpolluted, unconditioned. The source of creation holds potential in all children. The creative force offers a marvelous tool for children to fulfill their need to express themselves, to grow and to explore their world. Soon, however, through classes or criticisms, the notion of good and bad product is introduced into children's lives.

That notion generates a separation and a struggle between them and their creative play. When this middle step is interposed with its expectations, children are pressured into following rules and blueprints instead of their intuition. The true source of creation is abandoned and creative passion is lost. The connection is broken, and creativity becomes a mental activity; the children start to struggle for inspiration, and the pressure for achievement starts.

Creativity does not dwell just in the mystery; it is also very practical. When children learn to listen to themselves through creativity, they also learn to think for themselves and trust their feelings. Intuition is a wise, strong, and authentic voice that guides children to trust and express themselves. Intuition is the moving force of creativity; it is the fuel that maintains inspiration and brings about self-expression. Through the use of intuition, children become self-reliant; self-esteem and self-confidence develop, which enhance the way they respond to the world.

Children must discover that what they need to create is already inside them: an unlimited potential of play and inspiration. They must discover that they do not need to be taught everything and that creativity is a place without limits. The belief that they need models and instruction to create makes them dependent and uncertain about who they are and what they feel.

This is when parents, teachers, and other adults have a role to play. They can help preserve that endless source of passion in which children can explore anything about their world and their dreams without fear.

It is a great gift to children to show them how to use and respect their spontaneous intuition and to have them discover the magical surprises of creativity: a creativity that comes from a pure intimate source, deep within themselves.

SCHOOL AND THE HIDDEN AGENDA

What if I told you that those controlling public education policy actually have a hidden agenda? The goal of this agenda is to crush innovation, make children more obedient, and whatever else is needed in order to clip the wings of our children. To snip from them their natural creativity, curiosity, independence, freedom of thinking, and love of learning.

The true power behind education policy has never been educators or parents. The power lies with wealthy individuals and large corporations who want schools to help them train our children to obey authority, to find pleasure from material consumption, and to accept their rank in the economic food chain. Those in power want subservience and conformity, not creativity and freedom of thought. They seek obedient workers and pleasure seeking consumers that lack critical thinking skills, believe what they are told, and do not question authority. These are the people that profit from ignorance, and would lose control if our children were raised to think for themselves.

Yes, there has been research and innovation in education with new understandings of the human brain and progressive learner-centered approaches, but unfortunately the learner-centered revolution has quickly been put down and forgotten in the U.S., though it still thrives in expensive private schools, Montessori schools, and in nations like Finland. I also realize that there are teachers that have done their best to be creative and motivational, tried to fight against soul numbing policies, and tried to encourage students to enjoy learning. However, trying to enjoy learning and be creative in school for both teachers and students has been like trying to stop the wind from blowing the Autumn leaves from the trees.

My core message here is that instead of standardizing education we must personalize it.

By the time students reach high school they hate
school and cannot wait to finish an acceptable level of education and establish careers and families, imitating the suburban lifestyles of their parents. I believe that in an ideal school there would be no grades or tests. Teachers would not be cops or dictators. Schools would have fewer desks and more open space. Homework would be eliminated, and real teaching and dialogue would fill the day. Formulaic writing would be replaced by journaling.. Standardized tests would be replaced with portfolios of best work and art.

What can we do about this problem? For starters, it would help to have a sense of how the big lie of education is a part of the larger agenda of corporations and the wealthy attempting to crush independence, entrepreneurialism and democracy. Controlling children and dumbing down education has been going on for a very long time.

To really change things we to take back our power by educating ourselves and our children, wake each other up, ignite the flame of change, and challenge the criminals that have profited from obedience, conformity, and ignorance. By collaborating with one another, we have the power to take control over learning once again. We can give our children complete autonomy over their education, encourage self direction, deep critical thinking, and creativity. They are here to connect the dots and we are here to facilitate and instill in them the understanding that certain adults in positions of power are trying to manipulate and control them, for only that understanding will set them free.

THE NATURAL LOVE OF LEARNING

"The child is curious. He wants to make sense out of things, find out how things work, gain competence and control over himself and his environment, and do what he can see other people doing. He is open, perceptive, and experimental. He does not merely observe the world around him. He does not shut himself off from the strange, complicated world around him, but tastes it, touches it, hefts it, bends it, breaks it. To find out how reality works, he works on it. He is bold. He is not afraid of making mistakes. And he is patient. He can tolerate an extraordinary amount of uncertainty, confusion, ignorance, and suspense. ... School is not a place that gives much time, or opportunity, or reward, for this kind of thinking and learning."

-John Holt, *How Children Learn*

When left alone, children know instinctively which ways are best for them to learn. Peaceful and observant parents soon learn that it is safe and appropriate to trust this knowledge. These parents say to their baby, "Oh, wow! You're learning how to crawl in reverse!" They do not say, "That's the wrong way." Perceptive parents are aware that there are many different ways to learn, and they trust their children to know which are best for them.

Unschooling children are free from the intimidation of public embarrassment and failing, and keep their mind open to new exploration. Children learn not by answering questions, but by asking them. Schools teach children to hide one's ignorance about a subject than to learn more about it, regardless of one's curiosity. There is no need to motivate children through a reward system, such as high grades or gold stars. This suggest to the child that the activity must be difficult or unpleasant. Why is a reward, which has nothing to do with the subject at hand being offered? The conscious parent says, "I think you will enjoy this book", not "If you read this book, you will get a cookie."

No parent would tell their child, "Let's put that kitty down and get back to your book about cats." Unschoolers learn directly about the world. Our daughter describes unschooling as "learning what you want instead of what you're told." Ironically, the most common objection about unschooling is that children are "being deprived of the real world."

Family cohesiveness is perhaps the most meaningful benefit of the unschooling experience. Just as I saw her first step and heard her first word, I have had the privilege of hearing her read her first book all on her own, and sharing my daughter's world and her thoughts. Over the years, I have discovered more from her about life, learning, and love, than from any other source.

Sometimes I wonder who learns more in unschooling families. We learn along side one another and experience that growth and personal development as a family. It is the most incredible thing I could imagine having the privilege to do as a mother. As parents, we understand how difficult it is for children to learn something when they are rushed, threatened, or given a bad grade. When children think badly, perceive badly, when they are anxious or afraid, learning stops dead in its tracks.

Natural learners do not need structure. Unschoolers regularly surpass their schooled peers on academic achievement, socialization, confidence, and self-esteem. The success of self-directed learning strongly suggests that structured approaches inhibit learning and personal development. Self-directed, natural learners retain the curiosity, enthusiasm, and love of learning that every child is born with.

DESCHOOLING

In order for unschooling to work for us, I had to go through my own dark and difficult deschooling process. I had all these preconceived notions about what school is suppose to look like and how learning is suppose to happen. Deschooling is the process one goes through after leaving an institutionalized schooling environment. Your child has probably had their natural desire to learn squashed and will need time to recover from that. With our help they can get that love back and begin to see the world as a place where learning is gratifying and happening all of the time.

I often hear about many parents taking their kids out of school only to recreate the same forced learning environment at home, only to have it come to a crashing halt with the parent feeling like a failure and the kids being miserable. My husband Jeremy and I started reading unschooling authors and bloggers even before removing our children from school. That was the beginning of my deschooling. I started to become self-aware of my thoughts about school, and I started to question those thoughts. We often accept things without question simply because "that's the way it's always been done."

In school I had always been a "good" student. I did what I was told and made decent grades. I wasn't picked on, I had friends and got along with the teachers. I remember having to take a shop class in junior high school. I hated it and got a very low grade on my report card. There it was, in black & white…I failed at building things. Surprise, surprise…today, I hate putting anything together and have no confidence in my ability to make anything without it falling apart. I can barely hammer a nail. (Although this serves me well because Jeremy does 99% of these things).

Someone, who never met me, decided it was time for me to learn to build, and because

I wasn't interested at that time and found it boring, I was labeled "poor" in building. I never gave it any thought until I started deschooling. It wasn't like it crushed me when I got my report card. Rather it confirmed that the reason I must have found the class boring was because I wasn't good at it.

I started questioning why we allow the school system to continue having control over our children when the school day ends. Teachers give out lists of things for children to do at home. I've heard many parents tell their kids "You can't go out or play until you do your homework". What if this homework is interfering with family plans? Why are they telling our children what to do when they're in their own home on their own time? Why should families be expected to live by school policy at home? Schooled children come home the day before standardized tests, and let their parents know that they need to eat a good breakfast the next morning. And then hand them a list of what exactly the school's version of a good breakfast consists of. Why does the school system think they can dictate what parents and children do at home? Because we let them!

Once these thoughts started whirling around in my mind, there was no going back to my old way of thinking. I am now more aware of other people's thoughts about learning and education. Soon after we started out unschooling journey we ran into a friend and her daughter. It was close to the end of the school year and she asked if we "take a break for the summer". I explained that we learn all the time and that life is learning. I went on to say that it would be like taking a break from breathing. As they walked away I heard her say to her son , "See, they have to do school work every single day, even in summer!". *sigh*

I have even been asked how my kids do P.E. without being in school. Since when should anyone depend on the public school system for physical activity? It's as if physical activity is only a subject to be taken just at times that the school dictates. Ridiculous!

I also read a lot of John Holt during that first year of deschooling. I read almost every blog on unschooling I could find online and I could feel my thoughts and perspective changing as I read more and more.

My deschooling is a work in progress. I've learned so much about myself that it became more of a spiritual awakening than anything related to school. School seems like a foreign language to me now. I see what REAL learning is everyday with my children.

It looks nothing like school.

LEARNING THROUGH PLAY

Years ago when my eight year old daughter Callie was three I was under the impression that "early-intervention" was so important and that it was ideal for your child to be able to walk, talk, write, and read faster than all the other children and if they were behind then I would be labeled a failure. I heard parents talking about how when Kindergarten started the kids that didn't attend pre-school "didn't even know how to hold a pencil"! I found myself so proud that she seemed to be "ahead" and doing so well. She went to pre-k for two years and then Kindergarten at public school.

By the time she reached first grade she was burned out, already tired of school and learning. She was tired and depressed already. She wasn't learning to read. She said everyone was taking tests on tablets and she couldn't even take the test because she couldn't read the questions. She had a giant binder full of a bunch of unnecessary paperwork and wastes of paper and ink her teacher never filled out. The only thing the teacher ever had remarks on was whether or not they had a happy face or sad face and a reading score that was somehow declining over time. Regrettably, our first thought was that there had to be something wrong with our child. Her doctor put her on medication that turned her into a zombie.

She acted as if we had given her speed and got very ill. Three days later I vowed to never give her anything like that ever again and I started researching. I researched homeschooling methods. I had never even heard of unschooling. My first thought was that it sounded like a "lazy" method, and although it made sense I just couldn't grasp how it could possibly "work". My daughter has been thriving through unschooling. After a few months of playing games like Minecraft and getting interested in art, comic books, and manga she started reading. She taught herself over time because she wanted to be able to read, communicate, and connect with others and the world. When I heard her read a page from an actual book on her own I nearly cried. She loves reading, video games, and art. I'm so happy that we made the decision to transition to unschooling with her when we did.

On the other hand I'm fortunate that Hannah, who is three, is being unschooled from the very beginning and we are never looking back! She's already a very inquisitive child who loves learning new words and playing with colors and numbers. The things Callie was taught in preschool and had to practice practice Hannah picks up on naturally and effortlessly on her own. Everything she has learned she has through play, and big sister is now doing the same thing right along with her.

I can see them playing and actively engaged in an astonishing form of learning, and efficiently reaching by themselves things that would take hours with planned lessons. An interest sparks and suddenly they are very busy and full of ideas. They ask questions and spend hours, days, weeks, or even months learning about a topic. They draw, paint, read, etc all about their interest. They use their imagination and they often like to talk to others about it. You see growth and development when before they may have not been interested. They ask questions that you think would be beyond their understanding at that point. They amaze you and you see that there is more than one way to approach things. Eventually they will satisfy their curiosity and stop, until next time. At times the same interests appear again with times in between where it seemed like they were barely interested, and yet when they start again they are ahead of where they were before, subsequently learning and consolidating all that information in the space between ideas.

It's inspiring to watch the way my kids learn, the excitement in their eyes, and the sense of achievement. I am grateful that we are allowed this freedom. This is something I never want to take from them. Their natural desire to learn and their passion is contagious.

"Children do much of their learning in great bursts of passion and enthusiasm. They rarely learn on the slow, steady schedules that schools make for them. They are more likely to be insatiably curious for a while about some particular interest, and to read, write, talk and ask questions about it for hours a day and for days on end. Then suddenly they may drop that interest and turn to something completely different, or even for a while seem to have no interests at all. This usually means that for the time being they have all the information on that subject that they can digest, and need to explore the world in a different way, or perhaps simply get a firmer grip on what they already know."

-John Holt, *How Children Learn*

LEARNING TO TRUST

"All I am saying in this book can be summed up in two words: Trust Children. Nothing could be more simple, or more difficult. Difficult because to trust children we must first learn to trust ourselves, and most of us were taught as children that we could not be trusted."
                    -John Holt, *How Children Learn*

Since most of us were not unschooled ourselves we may have many fears about our own competence to create a rewarding learning environment. These fears are based on the our inexperience with unschooling as well as on the false assumptions about learning that our school experiences taught us years ago. When the present generation of unschooling children become parents themselves, they will have more confidence and trust in the process.

I feel that today's generation of parents have it the hardest, because we have to trust a process that we never experienced directly.

Trust is so very important. It's hard in the beginning (we're still learning to do this), but it's important to trust that our children can learn on their own, with minimal guidance, and that if they're interested in something, they'll learn about it. Don't get overwhelmed by the assumption that everything is in your hands. There is no need for us to choose the topics of the day. The best way to facilitate learning is to let them have the reins. They will naturally know what is of most interest to them at every moment, and will make that clear to you. Trust that your child knows best what they are ready and eager to learn, and then help them to find whatever materials or information they need. Relax and let your child take the lead. Once this concept is fully understood, unschooling becomes easy and fun.

EVERY WAKING HOUR

This is not your traditional, obligatory, stare-at-the-clock-until-the-bell-rings kind of learning. We are a growing movement of unschoolers who believe a force fed diet of standardized testing and indoor inactivity is choking the creativity out of our kids, and it's up to us to set 'em free.

This is exactly what I want for my daughters: freedom. Not just physical freedom, but intellectual and emotional freedom from the conventional learning that exists in our schools. I want for them the freedom to immerse themselves in the fields and forest that surround our home, to wander aimlessly or with purpose. I want them to remain free of social pressures to look, act, or think any way but that which feels most natural to them.

Children do life and in doing so gain knowledge. This naturally happens during every waking hour. Unschooling does not mean that we never teach anything to our children, or that our children should learn about life entirely on their own without our help and guidance. Unschooling does not mean that parents give up active participation in the education and development of their children and simply hope that something good will happen. Finally, since many unschooling families have definite plans for college, unschooling does not even mean that children will never take a course in any kind of a school.

We are unschoolers and we do things, not because we hope they will be good for us, but because they are fantastically interesting. There is an energy that comes from this that you can't get out of a curriculum. My children do things all day in a trusting and supportive home environment. Ironically, the people who are posting all of the "yes the kids are back in school" memes every fall are the ones that have the misconception that unschoolers are lazy. This is something that I work hard to do with my family every waking hour. Most people don't get out of bed in the morning in the mood for a "learning experience", I try to wake up every day in the mood for life. Children also do this - unless they are ill or life has been made overly stressful or confusing for them.

Unschooling is a unique opportunity for our family to do whatever makes sense for our personal growth and development. It's like watching a little garden grow. No matter how closely you watch your garden, it is difficult to verify that anything is happening at that very moment. But with the changing of the seasons we can see that much has happened, quietly and naturally. All we have to do is trust in the inevitability of this very organic process, and to facilitate that growth.

As unschoolers, we function outside the domain of the schools, and our philosophies and methods are not always understood, therefore assumptions are often made that we somehow lack awareness of our children's progress, and therefore require formal evaluation of that progress. So, how do we know our children are learning? The answer is simply, through direct observation.

We have two children. If a teacher had only two children in their classroom, and was unable to describe their reading skills, everyone would be appalled - how could a teacher have such close daily contact with only two kids and miss something so obvious? Yet many people unfamiliar with unschooling imagine that parents with just this sort of close daily contact with their child require outside evaluation to determine that child's progress. This puzzles unschooling parents, who cannot imagine missing anything so interesting as the nature of their child's learning.

None of the unschooling parents I know have twenty-five children, and we are free to focus on the enhancement of learning without being distracted by time-consuming tasks, unrelated to learning, that are necessary in a classroom. This freedom from distraction is a major factor in the establishment of a spirited, inventive, and blissful environment to learn.

Any parent of a toddler could almost certainly tell us not through testing, how many numbers her child can count to, and how many colors they know, but simply through many hours of listening and observing. This observation continues on into higher ages and more complex learning.

My children are naturally curious and ask many questions over the course of a day. They ask the meaning of words. If your child's self-esteem is intact, they will not hesitate to ask the meaning of these words. As an unschooling parent you can start to see when simply reading words is progressing in the direction of literacy. This may seem to outsiders to be somewhat imprecise, but unschooling parents learn through experience that more specific evaluation is invasive, unnecessary, and self-defeating.

If the government established mandatory testing for babies to determine whether they were walking on schedule, everyone would think that was ludicrous. We all know that healthy babies walk eventually, and that it would be futile and frustrating to attempt to speed up that process - as absurd as trying to speed up the blooming of a flower. Gardeners do not worry about late-blooming flowers, or measure their daily growth - they trust in nature, meet the needs of their plants, and know that any further intervention would interfere with the natural flow of their growth. This trust is just as essential in the education of a child as it is in gardening. All healthy flowers bloom when ready, all healthy babies walk when ready, and all healthy children in a family of readers read when ready. Some children may not read until they are ten or twelve. There is no need to speed up this process. When a child is free to learn at their own pace, they will continue to love learning throughout life.

So, as unschooling parents, if we do not measure, evaluate, and control learning, then how can our children know when to move on to the next level? Look at it this way. If we asked a horticulturist how a rose knows when to bloom, they couldn't give us an answer. We can simply assume that this knowledge is built into the wonderful genetics of the seed. The schedule of intellectual growth within our children is like the blooming rose. It may be a mysterious process, but it nevertheless exists within each child.

Callie, at eight-years-old, interestingly enough is already fascinated with politics and talks with everyone about it. How could I have guessed that she was ready for that level of understanding at this time in her life? Had I been imposing a standard curriculum, I might have discouraged this and emphasized reading or math, and to what end? Others disregard the fact that she is vastly knowledgeable and humanistic about social science, economic issues, government, and corruption. Instead they complain that I'm not forcing her to learn common core math.

As John Holt once observed, children are not trains. If a train does not reach every station on time, it will be late reaching its ultimate destination. But a child can be late at any "station", and can even change the entire route of the learning process, and still reach every area of learning.

The unschooling child not only knows what they need to learn, but how best to go about learning it. Callie has always devised ingenious ways for learning what is currently sparking her interest. My child is not unique; many unschooling parents have reported just this sort of enthusiasm, creativity, and joyful learning in their children as well. We don't give her lessons in the conventional sense on what she is interested in. She has taught herself, with help as needed and requested by her. "Subjects" are not treated as separate categories, but as parts of the topic of current interest.

I am not a teacher or a passive observer. I'm a facilitator. When she asks questions - which she does many times each day, her father and I answer as best as we can. If we can't, then we become researchers: We make phone calls, help her find sources on the Internet, take her to the library, or find someone with relevant experience with whom she can learn.

While we did not choose unschooling for religious reasons, we have always welcomed the time available to think, meditate, explore questions of spirituality, personal ethics, and to encourage such qualities as kindness, honesty, trust, cooperation, creative solutions to problems, and compassion for others. We have also appreciated having time in the morning to discuss such things as dreams from the previous night and plans for the day ahead, when we would otherwise be getting ready for school. Believing that modern life is already overly hectic, and living in an age of "information explosion," we try as much as possible to make room for deliberate and peaceful time with our family.

I think that it is no longer meaningful or realistic to require memorization of specific facts. These facts are essentially meaningless to the child unless they happen to coincide with their own current and unique interests. If your child learns how to obtain information, they can apply that skill all throughout life. As John Holt wrote, "Since we can't know what knowledge will be most needed in the future, it is senseless to try to teach it in advance. Instead, we should try to turn out people who love learning so much and learn so well that they will be able to learn whatever needs to be learned."

WHAT ABOUT COLLEGE?

Can unschoolers go to college? Most definitely! If your child aspires to be a doctor or lawyer a college degree is necessary. It all depends on what they want to do. There are benefits to college: you do learn a lot in college, and you take some time to figure out who you are and what you're interested in, and you make friends and develop a network that can last a lifetime. However, the real reason many kids go to college isn't because it's necessary, but because it's safe. They are afraid to go into the real world, so college becomes an easy thing to do before they have to get a job. I think this is wrong, because you're just wasting four years, and if you started with a job or creating your own business you'll be much better off than if you'd waited four years. I also think it's wrong to spend thousands and thousands of dollars or drowning in student debt.

Second, while it's true that college provides some benefits like a network of friends and time to figure out who you are, you don't need college to do this. In college, this stuff is provided to you, handed on a platter, and you don't need to figure things out. But figuring things out for yourself is really valuable. My belief is that college is not necessary for many people anymore. That wasn't as true when I was a kid but the world has changed drastically. Now many extraordinary jobs and businesses can be had without a college degree. In fact, I would argue that real-world experience is vastly superior to a degree, and a degree is too expensive compared to the benefits for many people. Artists, photographers, writers, musicians, videographers, etc. don't need a degree. Programmers can learn their skills online. Computer science degrees are nice, from what I understand, but not necessary. You can learn 3D animation, web design, or UI online. Many people with MBA's say their degrees are almost worthless. My best friend is a chef, and he said his culinary school degree isn't necessary, and in fact was incredibly expensive. He advises my daughter to not go to culinary school, but to get real-world experience instead.

There are many alternatives to going to college. If you have money aside to pay for your child's college, what if you paid the same amount (or less) for them to start their own business or create their own thing? This would be a better learning experience than partying for four years in college. Parents often pay for room and board, along with tuition. What if you paid for room and board outside of college, and some money to start a business? Do interesting things. Learn. Share it with people. Sell something. Find yourself in the process. Encourage your child to start a business. Even if they do go to college. Or at least encourage them to start creating something they love.

They can write a screenplay, start a Youtube channel, write a book or blog, create some websites or programs. Start these things with your child as soon as you can, and teach yourself and your child what you need to know to succeed. The possibilities are endless. Make friends and encourage your children to make friends. Making friends in college is really valuable, but you can make them online, meet them in person, and work on things together. Find a co-founder. Do a project together. Travel and meet people. All of these things could be a lot more valuable, could cost way less than college, and make you more employable in less time than someone who comes out of college with a degree and little to no experience.

WHAT IS CONSCIOUS PARENTING?

Conscious parenting is a peaceful parenting approach that gives a wider understanding of the dynamics between parent and child. As unschooling parents we want to approach parenting challenges in a more constructive way than traditional parenting styles. It's important for us to be aware of the example we are setting through our responses to our children and the importance of trying to meet the underlying needs that may be driving their behavior.

This contrasts with traditional parenting styles which often focus on the child's behavior, often using punishment and isolation as a strategy for modifying behavior. A system of punishments, threats, or rewards may work in the short term, adopting a punishment-free approach is a fundamental factor in establishing relationships that are based on trust and mutual respect, for creating a healthy morale in the family.

The Conscious Parenting approach fosters more willing cooperation, integrity and self-discipline in children over time as their natural development allows as opposed to obedience based on fear. This non-threatening, connection based parenting approach is based on past and current attachment research and at it's core is the acknowledgment that to bring about long lasting positive change, parents need to gain a better understanding of what their child needs in their growth and development.

A parent gaining a greater awareness of their child's attachment and developmental needs leads to a greater motivation to learn the parenting tools which hold the value of the parent child relationship at the core. This change needs to happen first on an emotional level. Peaceful parenting puts balanced focus on helping parents develop self-awareness and self-regulation, self-growth, self-healing, mindfulness and meditation.

Peaceful parenting without punishment is essential when supporting the child to make choices from a place of integrity, self-discipline and self-responsibility rather than fear of disapproval or desire for reward. Creating a culture of mutual respect, empathy and respectful listening, sensitivity to each person's feelings and problem solving all help to foster communication in the family that's based more on love, respect and compassion. So, not only is there an alternative to punishment, it's the only alternative that leads to long term peace and harmony in families and effectively meets children's needs for emotional safety, security, developing emotional intelligence and unconditional love.

Conscious parenting is based on clear and patient communication and trust in the child's basic goodness. Instead of raising our voice or inserting a threat, make physical contact, come down to their level, touch them kindly, calmly get their attention, be clear about your expectations and ask them what is wrong. Adopting mutual problem-solving skills to lifts both the adult and child out of the power struggle. This approach teaches parents to relate primarily to the feelings beneath the behavior and to respond primarily to those feelings. This helps children learn to identify their own feelings and increases their emotional literacy.

This is different from many traditional parenting approaches which focus on changing a child's behavior using techniques that involve time-out and creating artificial consequences for the child which tends to cause children to feel stressed, defensive, rejected and rebellious. These responses create a tense and emotionally insecure environment for children to live and learn in. This tension causes children to feel stressed, insecure, rejected, and greatly increases their tendency to be resistant, rebellious and reactive.

One of the most profound ways that children learn is by mirroring our behavior. When we use manipulation, threats, bribes or punishments, we are teaching them that this is what they should do and how they should be in relationships. Consequently, this will become their default mode in attempting to make others act the way they want them to act. In other words, they will naturally think and feel in terms of manipulating, bribing, threatening and punishing.

Aggressive behavior and "whining" are most likely signs of unmet needs. The child may be hungry, exhausted, overstimulated, or they may have a need to release their pent up stresses and frustrations. It may well be an indication that there's too much chaos and the child is feeling disconnected, defensive or overwhelmed. As peaceful parents we're always seeking to explore what the underlying needs may be that are driving the behavior.

When we give children the safety and permission to feel and express their feelings, children can return to balance and again live happily in the moment. When children are emotionally safe and calm, they can give their full attention and enthusiasm to their play and learning. However, a child who carries a collection of invalidated and unreleased tears and fears is less available mentally and emotionally and will be frustrated which manifests in resistant behavior.

Parents have emotional needs too. Our need for emotional support and release is just as big and just as valid as our child's. We have to take care of ourselves first. Although we endeavor to parent with patience and kindness, we also must understand that putting the principle into practice is not always easy. It's unfair to "expect" ourselves as parents to just be calm and non-critical especially since we have quite a lot of processing of our own emotional scars going on. It is important that we have the opportunity and support to meet our own emotional needs and practice self-love so that we can move in a more positive direction with our parenting.

If life were easy I guess it would be boring. I try to live a deliberate life. Living in the present and free from expectation is the goal. I've experienced so much growth in recent years, and I still keep finding new ways to love myself. While I try to live with little to no regrets, I have definitely done things I'm not proud of. Reminding myself that every decision made has brought me to where I am today, definitely helps. Self love is all about motivating yourself and remembering that one day your actions will all make sense. The pain and hurt will be worth it. People's thoughts of you will be insignificant. And the people you decide to surround yourself with will be next to you through your entire journey.

Similarly, I've struggled with learning to let go and instead look forward. Accepting life for exactly what it is. Self love and care is something that I've had to teach myself for quite a while now but I've mastered the various ways in which I can recharge and recenter while I restore my mental health. For me, a hot bath with a hot cup of coffee (or Mascato) is a great place for me to completely relax. I put my phone out of reach with a movie or listen to my favorite playlist. This helps to block the noise and stresses of life for a moment.

Comparison is the thief of happiness – SO DON'T! Look up to others without bringing yourself down. Be mindful when comparing yourself to someone else. If I ever catch myself comparing, I immediately stop and feed myself some positivity. Positive affirmations are your new best friends! Self-care is NOT selfish! Take care of your mind, body, and soul. Self-care can be practiced through things like exercising, meditating, getting enough sleep, diet, etc. Eliminate toxicity in your life. It's that simple… if it isn't nourishing your mind, body, or soul, get rid of it!

I've also been teaching myself not to take everything so personally. Forgive, move on and let stuff remain in the past. That one has taken me quite a few years of therapy and other such remedies, but deep down I've learned control and how to keep calm. *shoutout to the best friend!!!*

"May your coffee be stronger than your toddler"

A WILDSCHOOLING ADVENTURE

The world is yours, so get it! Unschooling, Wildschooling, Worldschooling, Wanderschooling. These are a few terms in which many unschooling families use to describe our many adventures. Why is adventure so important to unschooling families? Children (and adults) benefit from their experiences with nature. By exposing children to the outside world and all that nature has to offer, you are opening their eyes to new challenges and experiences.

There are so many other cognitive, physical, and social benefits to getting outside. Not only can the great outdoors reduce stress, helping them to maintain better mental health, but it is also a great way to help maintain a more physically well-being, which also encourages a more psychologically well-being as well. When enjoying the outdoors, many people are often enjoying it in groups, encouraging the development of essential life skills such as teamwork, communication, and relationship building. It is also plays an influential role in establishing a sense of belonging and self-worth. In more recent times, nature has been replaced by technology. Technology is great, but it is important that we, as parents, are encouraging our family to get outside. Some of the best ways to do this is by backpacking, bike rides, rock climbing, or simply going on a nature hike.

Jeremy and I met at our first job in high school, and we were both in the military when we were younger. We're just a couple of wandering souls with two incredible and insane offspring with wanderlust. At this time we are stuck in central Alabama in a tiny apartment and are in the process of rebuilding our farm house that burned down this past summer and are sort of living in limbo, but hoping to get over that soon. Alabama is a bit boring, but isn't so bad. We're close to Birmingham so the art and music scene is pretty rad. We're close enough to the beach and also not too far from the Smoky Mountains. We try to take a vacation every year, but things have been rough since our house fire. Hopefully in the next few years we will be able to travel more! We have maps and lists of all the places we want to visit. Callie wants to take a trip to Disney World when Star Wars Land opens in a few years. Being a theater kid she of course also has big plans for Broadway. I love having the freedom to go on these amazing adventures with my family. Of course schooled families can also do these things, but

I'm not going to lie. There is something so peaceful about going to the beach and it being empty because most everyone else is stuck in school. Most of the adventures that we go on are local. The woods near our house, lakes, nature preserves. Alabama has some beautiful mountains, streams, waterfalls, and even caves! We consider nearly everything an adventure. Trips to the dentist or the local farmers market. There is something to be learned all of the time!

PARENT RESOURCES

Unschool Rules- **http://unschoolrules.com/** (One of my favorite sites for breaking down subjects (for my public school-taught brain)

Family Unschoolers Network- **http://www.unschooling.org/**

The Unschooler Experiment- **http://www.podcastchart.com/podcasts/the-unschooler-experiment-podcast**

Learning in Freedom- **http://learninfreedom.org/**

Radical Unschooling- **http://unschoolers.org/radical-unschooling/what-is-radical-unschooling/**

Sandra Dodd- **http://sandradodd.com/unschooling**

Dayna Martin- **http://daynamartin.com/**

Living Joyfully- **http://livingjoyfully.ca/**

AHA! Parenting-
http://www.ahaparenting.com/

Unschooling Mom2Mom-
http://www.unschoolingmom2mom.com

Free Range Kids-
http://www.freerangekids.com/

Freedom to Learn-
http://www.freedomtolearnproject.com/

John Holt- **http://www.johnholtgws.com/**
Sir Ken Robinson-
http://sirkenrobinson.com/

Stone Age Techie-
http://stoneagetechie.blogspot.com/

Stories of an Unschooling Family-
**https://www.storiesofanunschoolingfamily.
com/**

The Natural Child Project-
http://www.naturalchild.org/

The Orange Rhino-
http://theorangerhino.com/

The Unschooling Blog Carnival-
**http://unschoolingblogcarnival.blogspot.co
m/**

Here you can access many different blogs. It's
a great way to see real life examples of others
who have embraced the unschooling method
of learning!

ONLINE SITES FOR KIDS

Minecraft Homeschool-
http://www.homeschoolwithminecraft.com/

I can't say enough good things about this
online Minecraft Homeschool. They have
taken this popular game and turned it into an
amazing way to learn about history! Love it.

Typing for Kids-
https://www.typingclub.com/

I really love this program and how fun they make typing for kids!

Starfall- http://www.starfall.com/

Online learning and games just for kids!

Coursera- https://www.coursera.org/ free online courses.

Khan Academy-
https://www.khanacademy.org/

Their mission is to provide a free, world-class education for anyone, anywhere. All of their resources are completely free.

Open Culture- http://www.openculture.com/ such a powerful collection of free learning resources, including a list of free online college courses, language learning, and more.

Shmoop- https://www.shmoop.com/ an exciting way to learn literature and history.

Self-Made Scholar- http://selfmadescholar Free classes and resources for self-education.

Zinn Education Project- https://zinnedproject.org/ excellent resources for learning history, Howard Zinn style

Free Rice- http://freerice.com/#/english- vocabulary/1417 game for learning different subjects.

OUTSIDE ACTIVITIES

Hiking
Swimming
Hunting and Fishing

Biking
Sports
Cloud watching
Geocaching
Wildlife Photography
Tracking
Local 4-H Club
Gardening

CRAFTS, PROJECTS, SUBSCRIPTIONS

- **http://www.DIY.org**

Make:Projects- **http://www.makezine.com**

Lowe's and Home Depot free Saturday workshops

Green Kids Crafts Pinterest Board- **https://www.pinterest.com/greenkidcrafts/**

DIY.org

Green Kid Crafts Subscription Program-
https://www.greenkidcrafts.com/ this is a great
resource for parents who don't like search for
craft ideas and gather all the supplies for crafts.
Every month, you are shipped a Discovery
Box of ready to make crafts!

Some other fun subscription boxes : Kiwi
Crate, Tinker Crate, Koala Crate, Amazon
Stem Toy Club, History Unboxed, Groovy Lab
in a box, Spangler Science Club, Ivy Kids,
Junior Explorors, Bitsbox, Little Tinker Box,
Creation Crate, Magic Schoolbus, Little
Passports Family,

Snack Crates- includes snacks and candies
from around the world. These are my kid's
personal favorite monthly subscription crates!
Munchpak, Candy Club, Nature Box, Vegan
Cuts Snack Box, Urthbox, Taste Trunk, Love
With Food Gluten Free Taste Box, Graze, Bear
Naked, Snack Sack, Freedom Japanese Market,
Fit Snack, Snack Nation, Treats, Korea Box,

Raw Box, Num-Nums Munch Box, Hey Gluten Free, Healthy Surprise, Carnivore Club, Universal Yums, Tiki Box, Oyatsu Box, Mexicrate, Candy Japan

NETWORKING, MEETING OTHER HOME(UN)SCHOOLERS IN YOUR COMMUNITY

Visit Libraries- When I go to the Library with my kids, I let them pick out what they want, and then I find a bunch of books that I think they'd be interested in and that make learning fun and stack them all together.

Extracurricular Activities are a great way for children to find their talent and what they love. My oldest has tried it all from softball to musical theater. She enjoys performing on stage and is now enrolled in an Acrobatic Dance Class. Little sis is still pretty shy, but she's decided to try a ballet and tap class. I can't wait to see them grow this year. Unschooling gives them the freedom to master their talents and work instead of being overwhelmed with school and homework. This has also been a way for us to meet other homeschooled children in our area.

Local Homeschooling and Unschooling Facebook Groups- I can't stress enough the importance of joining a homeschooling/unschooling group! You will be blown away at how many people in your community are home(un)schooling. It's not only a great support for parents to talk, but also for your children to make friends and to plan activities together. I'm in a few different local homeschooling groups and there are so many events we have to say no to many so we don't over schedule. There are some amazing people out there. Go connect with them and you just might find life-long friends! You can find me on Facebook!**http://www.Facebook.com/TheU nschoolMom**

Some of the Facebook Blogs I follow are:

https://www.facebook.com/theunschooldad/

https://www.facebook.com/UisforUnschooling/

https://www.facebook.com/happinessishereblog/

https://www.facebook.com/groups/UnschoolingMom2MomParenting/

https://www.facebook.com/singlemomunschooling/

https://www.facebook.com/unschoolrules/

I also do a lot of networking and get inspiration daily from unschooled families that I follow on Instagram. You can find me on Instagram. Here is think link to my Instagram and some other awesome unschooling instagram pages that I follow:

http://www.instagram.com/theunschoolmom

http://www.instagram.com/theunschooldad

http://www.instagram.com/gentleparenting _memes

http://www.instagram.com/ourwildblackbe rries

http://www.instagram.com/schoolin_reyes

http://www.instagram.com/theselflovefairy

http://www.instagram.com/familythathikes

http://www.instagram.com/theunschoolmo mmy

http://www.instagram.com/weirdcreativefa mily

http://www.instagram.com/sageparenting

http://www.instagram.com/holisticmama

http://www.instagram.com/kelleythalhamer

Made in the USA
Las Vegas, NV
25 January 2022